Conversations with my dog

About our journeys and finding the way home

First published 2022

Copyright © Hannah Gold 2022

The right of Hannah Gold to be identified as the author of this work has been asserted in accordance with the Copyright, Designs & Patents Act 1988.

All rights reserved. No part of this book may be reproduced, stored in a retrieval system, or transmitted in any form or by any means, electronic, electrostatic, magnetic tape, mechanical, photocopying, recording or otherwise, without the written permission of the copyright holder.

Published under licence by Brown Dog Books and The Self-Publishing Partnership Ltd, 10b Greenway Farm, Bath Rd, Wick, nr. Bath BS30 5RL

www.selfpublishingpartnership.co.uk

ISBN printed book: 978-1-83952-586-5
ISBN e-book: 978-1-83952-587-2

Illustrations by Hannah Gold
Cover and internal design by Andrew Prescott
Cover photo © Hannah Gold

Printed and bound in the UK

This book is printed on FSC® certified paper

Conversations with my Dog

About our journeys and finding the way home

Hannah Gold

This book is dedicated to Monty, my best friend and teacher, with whom I rediscovered the wonder of the Out There.

And to my friends Paquita and Paul who brought him into my life one unexpected, midwinter afternoon.

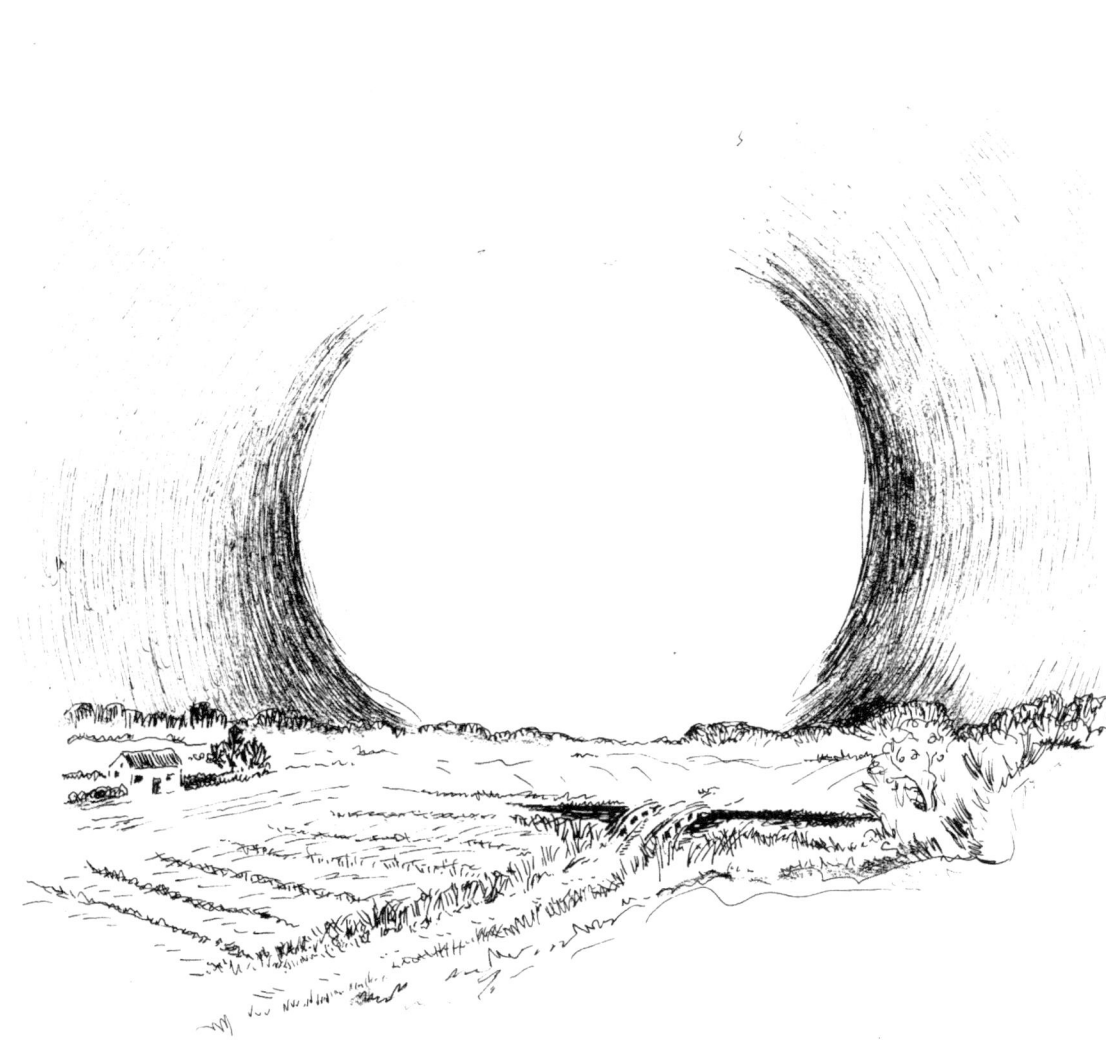

Introduction

It is often said that 'home is where the heart is', but recently I have come to think that it is more than that. Home is the place the heart makes us seek. It is the place that the person we have not yet become makes us stretch to find as if we somehow carry a forwards-echo of it even before knowing its outward face.

At the closing of an old year, the arrival in my life of my sweet friend, Monty, was followed closely by a convergence of circumstances that meant I found myself unexpectedly seeking a new place to live for us both and having to take him with me on many roads, all too frequently without any view of success in sight. My dear, loyal friend threw himself into all the challenges that the road ahead would bring, with a tenacity and enthusiasm that were a revelation to me. My 'little dog' was no longer a *little* dog but proved to be a huge spirit who just happened to be running around in a small furry body. Some of the most challenging months of my life have been flooded with gratitude for his unflappable friendship and natural wisdom.

On all our travels, Monty has been ceaselessly welcoming to new friends, despite the many fluctuations in his own life and open to sharing his loving personality freely everywhere we have been. He would walk up to people in new places, starting conversations and leaving a trail of cheerfulness behind him, even when I might not have bothered to say, 'Hi,' had he not been there. I grew to match him because I had to. He reassured me through difficult days and didn't stop there but did the same for my friends as well. Before long, I realised that, although he is 'my dog', his vast character is so enormous that there is more than enough to go around to not only dwarf any challenges our lives might face but also to make others happy along the way while we overcome them.

When worry threatened to absorb me, he told me of the values of simplicity, happiness and fun. When I felt lost he would look at me with joy, unfettered by false complexities and wiggle with grateful delight at the gift of a simple ball. "Wow! A BALL. Is that really for me? THANK YOU!" Between us we wrote and illustrated our conversations so that anyone who wants to can share his humour and ideas about life. This book is for anyone who may be wishing for an extra friend on their journey. Maybe you already know what it is to have a dog at your side. But, if not and you just wish for it, then even across whatever distances may appear to separate us in person, you do now. One thing Monty has taught me is how huge love is and how it dissolves all distances and separations.

Far back in the history of humans on Earth, our species was nomadic. We survived by following game and gathering wild food, moving to places which held what was important to us, according to the provisions of location and season. From our earliest ancestry around eight hundred thousand years ago, to as recently as eight or nine thousand years ago, we lived this way. Those millennia imprinted on the human psyche the command 'keep moving!' If you don't like where you are, move to a better place. To stagnate in one location is to stop being able to provide for yourself and those you care about and to die.

Somewhere along that long journey, humans and dogs started to fuse a partnership. We can't really be sure how long ago. All we can say is that our current evidence of the relationship goes back around fifteen thousand years. If it was longer we don't know. It could have been. By contrast, our transition from nomadic lifestyles to settled communities only took place around eight or nine thousand years ago. So, dogs became an integral part of human lives while we were still living nomadic hunter existences and our relationship with our canine companions is inherently rooted in the act of travelling and hunting together long before it became about protecting static places. Dogs joined their lives to those of humans as travellers significantly before we started to share a more territorial way of life. This is the earliest basis for their understanding of us. It was a perfect symbiosis. Dogs could alert us to the presence of game and approaching danger. We could offer them improved shelter, security and more reliable food supply. Life was dangerous, full of risk and opportunity. Dogs and humans improved each other's chances of survival.

Moving away from nomadic living has left an instinctive dichotomy deep in the human brain. A nomad understands that to remain in one place too long is to dwindle and die, because nowhere can sustain you in the long term. You must follow the herd and the seasons. You must not get left behind. A settled dweller learns to be rooted to a location because it provides what they need. People learned that if the triangle of life, shelter, water and food, plus the vital addition of a defensible position could be maintained in one place, there was no need to go. To travel was to take risk, to face losing what you had found, when it was comparatively comfortable. Since then, the competing nomad and settler within us have whispered in our subconscious brains the contrasting commands 'Go!' and 'Stay!' We still find ourselves torn by the impetus of each, even when we no longer recall their origins.

After a long and well-established period of what our society would deem a 'conventional' life, with a house, mortgage and good job, I suddenly found it could not sustain me and I became accidentally nomadic. I set out to move house. It should have been simple but it wasn't. My new place fell through, three times. Meanwhile, I had given up my house to my buyer. I had quit the job that I just couldn't bring myself to do any longer and was renting, with limited and rapidly dwindling resources. But this was about more than just leaving a job or moving house. I needed to find some reality again. Some 'real' reality, the kind with some truth in it. Monty said, "Whatever you are searching for, take me with you. I will help you find it!" And suddenly things were simple again.

Sometimes there are moments when the inner nomad insists on change and we just know we have to leave, wherever and whatever we were. Monty understood this. Dogs have been with us as travellers for far longer than they have been beside us as settlers. Together, we set off into the wilds of the unknown. When I said, "We're taking a chance here!" he replied, "Exploring is normal." When I looked ahead and doubted myself, he looked at the day with me and said, "Let's have an adventure!" His fearless friendship reminded me how to live. I learned not only to love but to respect him. Once I found enough humility to recognise that, just because I was the human didn't mean I knew more and realised that my part in our relationship was as the student rather than teacher, I started to watch and listen to him and then to the world around us again. Through his eyes I saw frosty moonlight, dawn on the river and misty fields. I remembered once again to listen to the calls of birds in the trees and the music of rain. I had thought I was setting out to find a new house. Instead, I found myself being rewilded by my dog and searching for the real meaning of home. I found myself rediscovering what it meant to know what was real again and questioning what was important, because it was clear that he already knew. His life was based around friendship, loyalty, exploration and fun. He never compromised these values.

Setting out to find a home, I found that there were bigger questions to be answered about what home and journeys really are. Through our travels, Monty, with his endless sense of adventure, taught me far more than what I had thought I needed to learn. The wild places that remain in all of us were suddenly speaking loud and clear again. The big 'Out There' was inviting us to step into it and grow, with the discovery of all types of new horizons. Monty and I offer some of our conversations to you, in the hope that they bring you inspiration and joy on your own adventures.

Welcome

"Welcome home, Monty!"
"Ooh! It's so exciting! What's 'Home'?"

"Home is where we are together. Home is a good thing. It's somewhere we play and cuddle and share food. You must always remember where Home is".

"OK. I'm tired out now. You're nice and warm. Can I have a snooze right he…re?
Zzz…"
"Of course you can."

Conversations with my Dog

"What's that outside the gate?"
"It's a field."
"Smells interesting. I think I like it."
"When you are a bit older, we can go play in it. There are lots of fields out there to play in"
"Really? Can we play in all of them?"
"We can have fun trying!"
"OK"

Conversations with my Dog

"Is there anything else out there?"
"Oh yes. There's a great big Out There, out there Monty! It's huge and we're going to see lots of it."
"Promise?"
"I promise. Now have a little sleep. You're still very young. The Out There will still be there waiting for us to explore."
 "It sounds very big."
  "It's so big we will never, ever get to the end of it. It's full of fields and interesting things to discover."
   "OK. I love you."
    "I love you too."

Conversations with my Dog

"Sometimes everything seems so complicated, Monty."
"Well maybe it seems that way, but all the really important things are simple. I love you. I'm yours and I love you. Remember that."
"I will."

Conversations with my Dog

"Love is not complicated. It requires no explanation. It just Is."

Conversations with my Dog

"We need to go on a journey today Monty"
"Good! Can we look for some adventures?"
"We certainly can. It's a longer journey than normal Monty, much further than just going for a walk."
"OK. Sounds like fun!"

Conversations with my Dog

"You know you like searching? Well we are going on a search."
"Great! What are we searching for?"
"We need to find a new home."
"Why?"
"Well, I've sold our one and we need to leave soon. I haven't found us a new one yet."

"I don't understand 'sold.'"
"Oh, right."

Conversations with my Dog

"Let's take Home with us."
"It doesn't really work that way."

"Why not? You told me that Home was somewhere we are together.
"Yes."
"I'm here. You're here. So that means we're home."
"I guess you're right."

"I still need to find us a physical home though. You know, somewhere with a roof and walls. Somewhere we go back to that's ours."
"Sounds like a den."
"Yes, I guess so."

"My home is where you are."
"I'm glad."

Conversations with my Dog

"I will build our home around you, Monty."
"I'm glad too."

Conversations with my Dog

"Where are we going to live, Monty?"

Conversations with my Dog

"Together."

Conversations with my Dog

"What do you do when you're scared and don't know what to do next Monty?"
"I cuddle you. You make everything good again. Didn't you know that?"
"I was hoping so."
"Well if you get scared you can just cuddle me. It works. It's what I'm here for! To love and cuddle you. And protect you."
"Protect me? You're a puppy."
"I'm your dog. It's why I'm here."

Conversations with my Dog

"You are very young to know why you are here."

"The very young always know why they are here. Because they haven't forgotten. Sometimes life muddles things up with too many thoughts. But the heart is ageless."

Conversations with my Dog

"Even when we are in small bodies, we have big spirits."

Conversations with my Dog

"So your job is to look after me – and my job is to look after you?"
"Yup."

"Anything else?"
"We have fun together."

"Anything else?"
"We eat biscuits."

Conversations with my Dog

"I'm here to teach you to have more fun. You're allowed to learn by having fun, like dogs do, not just the human ways like reading or doing difficult stuff."

Conversations with my Dog

"How about when things don't make sense?"
"I follow my nose. Try it!"
"I think I've forgotten how."
"That's OK. I can show you."
"Can you?"
"I'm your dog. It's what I'm here for."
"Oh. OK."

"I told you it was simple."
"Yes, you did. You're right."

"Sometimes I feel like I don't know how to sort all this out Monty!"
"I trust you."
"Why?"
"Because we're friends."

Conversations with my Dog

"Don't worry. I will bring you all my favourite things. Would you like an old shoe? Here, have one of my best toys! It always makes me feel better.

I tell you what, I've got a lovely bone… you can share it with me!"

"Thanks Monty. I feel better already!"

Conversations with my Dog

"I don't know what I will ever do without you Monty."
"That's silly. Why would you have to do without me?"
"Because nothing is forever. Humans, dogs, no-one lives forever."
"Friendship is forever and I'm your friend. Love is forever if we want it to be."

Conversations with my Dog

"But one day you won't be here. One day I won't be here."

"We will be somewhere. Even if it's somewhere else. You told me there's a great big Out There, out there, remember? So big that no-one can even find the end of it."

"Yes, I did."

"Well, don't you think, in the middle of all that Out There, we will be somewhere?"

"Yes, I do. At least, that's what I feel."

Conversations with my Dog

"Well, wherever you are, I will be there. Even if you go all the way to the very end of the Out There, I'm coming too!"

"You love me that much?"

"Yup."

"Why?"

"Because I'm your dog. I love you. I protect you. To protect you I will have to be there, so of course I will be. It's what dogs do. It's what friends do."

"When a dog gives it's heart, it is forever. Forever isn't bound by things like time and location. It is bigger than that."

"You've reminded me: a famous human scientist, called Einstein, once said that energy can neither be created nor destroyed."

"What's a scientist?"

"A clever person who thinks about things a lot and asks lots of questions."

"Cool. Do they have any biscuits?"

"Probably. Is that what you mean about the Out There? Us being out there in it somewhere else, some other time?"

"Yes. If it's really that big, then everything has to be out there somewhere, somewhen, right? So, like your scientist says, we can't really begin or end."

"So every cuddle there could ever be and every possible kind of biscuit has to be out there somewhere?"

"That's right. Now you're getting it. Let's go and find them all!"

"OK Monty. We can start right now."

Conversations with my Dog

"Humans have a word for that, Monty, they call it 'infinity.'"
"Infinite Tea?! I like the sound of that!"

"How do you know these things Monty?"
"We all know these things. Because the truth is in all of us. But sometimes we forget what we know. I just haven't forgotten."

"Why not?"
"Well, it helps that I'm a dog. It also helps that you are listening. When someone is surrounded by people who aren't listening to what they know then they will usually forget it sooner or later, just to fit in with the pack."

Conversations with my Dog

"Why would someone give up their own knowledge to fit in with the pack?"

"The pack spends a lot of time and effort digging in the dirt, jostling for position and hunting for scraps.

Sometimes we fit in just to be anywhere in the pack, not because we don't know how to survive outside it but because we never imagine knowing."

"But the things we knew won't go away?"

"If something is real then it is part of the Infinite Tea and that is everywhere, including in all of us. It can't go away because there is no 'away' for it to go to."

Conversations with my Dog

"I see what you mean. Buddhists have a saying, 'Be here, now!'"

"Well, I don't know what Buddhists are, but every thing is really here and now. Just sometimes it seems like it isn't. So if you are truly Here and Now then you are everywhere in the Infinite Tea. Maybe what they are saying is 'Be real!'"

"Buddhists understand about the Infinite Tea."

"Great. Do you think they like biscuits?"

"I'm pretty sure they would do, yes."

Conversations with my Dog

"I want to travel everywhere with you Monty. I wish I could see the world with you."

"We can."

"Well, my car won't take us to all those places. Sometimes we need things called aeroplanes."

"What are those?"

"Well, they are things that fly, that people travel a long way in. I can't take you on one of those."

"Oh, well let's not bother with those. We can fly without that!"

"We can? How?"

"When I dream, I fly! All we have to do is dream together."

"Those are dreams though. This is real."

"Real is a dream too. It's just a different way of dreaming. A different way to explore. One where it takes a little longer for the things we think to happen. The other dreams are faster… and we can fly in those."

Conversations with my Dog

"Life is about learning that, because we are real, we come from the Infinite Tea and are everywhere within it. We can go anywhere. All we have to do is dream differently. When we do that we can travel much further than our cars or our paws can take us."

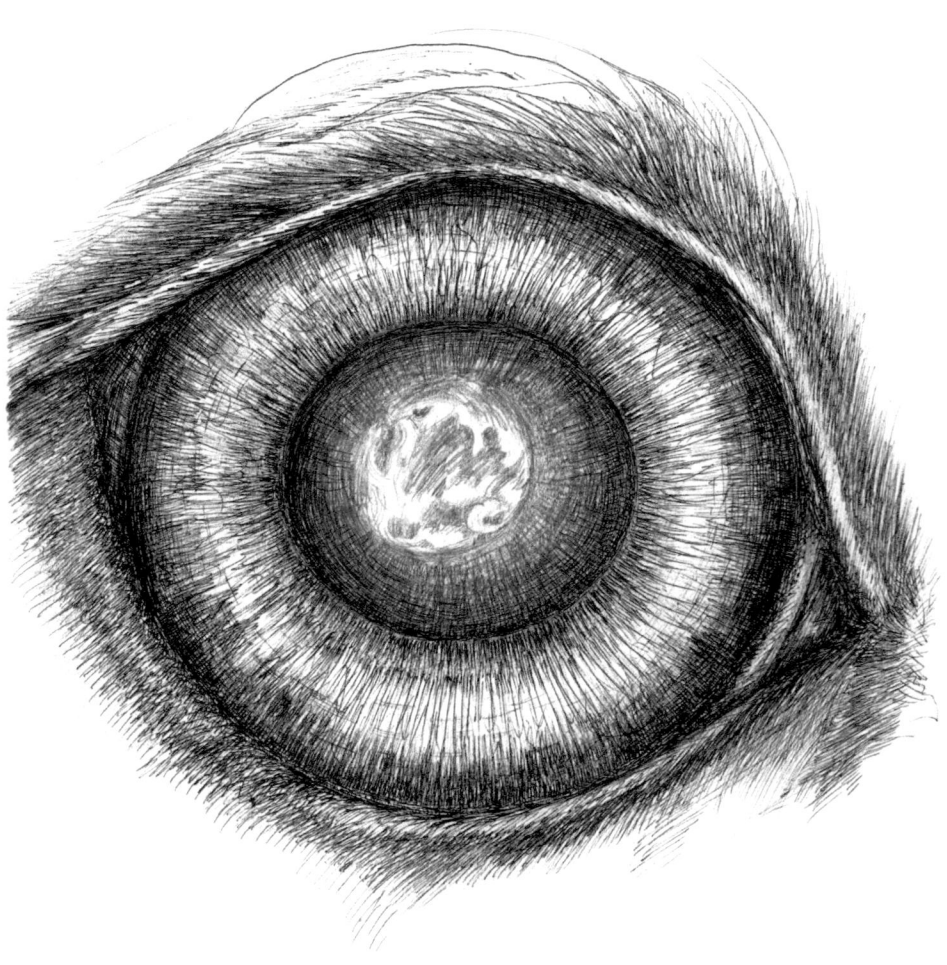

Conversations with my Dog

"Good morning! Good morning! Wake up! I'm excited!"
"Why are you so excited Monty?"

"Because it's morning! It's wonderful! And I love you! Can we go and play? Can we? Can we? Please! Take me for a walk! Take me out in the car! Can we go play in the Infinite Tea? Please, please please!!!"

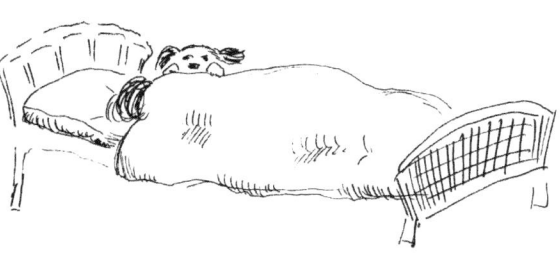

"OK Monty, let me get dressed."

"Why do you need to do that? Can't we just go right now?"
"Cos I'm a human and it's just something we do."
"OK."

Boing, boing, boing…

"You're happy today, Monty!"
"Of course I am. I love you. I'm here and you're here. There are adventures to find and fields to play in. Games to play! A whole huge Out There just waiting for us to explore it!"

"Are you always happy Monty?"
"I think so. Sometimes I get scared but I'm always happy, because even when I'm scared you are there to make things right, so I'm happy too. Mostly I'm just happy."

"So what would you say about how to be happy, Monty?"
"That's easy! Love and cuddles."

"That's it? Love and cuddles?"
"Yup… Oh and then biscuits!"

"Why in that order?"
"Well, because if I had love and cuddles but no biscuits, I would still be happy but I'd be hungry. But if I had lots of biscuits but no love and cuddles, I'd be really sad and even more empty inside than if I had no biscuits. Having no love is a bigger kind of emptiness."

"I know you are really good at sniffing out biscuits, but how do you find love and cuddles, Monty?"

"Well what I do is give them away free to anyone who wants them. Then you get them back. It's kind of a growing thing, a bit like a tree. When you share them it makes more. I've noticed that doesn't work with biscuits."

"You can make a lot of things better with a biscuit, but you can put even more right with love. When I got a thorn in my paw, I didn't want a biscuit, I wanted love and a cuddle so you could put it right. A biscuit can't make my paw better."

Conversations with my Dog

"Biscuits are great but they have some limitations. Love has no limits."

Conversations with my Dog

"I think some humans could learn a lot from you, Monty."
"Why is that?"

"Just seems to me like they spend too much time hunting for their biscuits."
"Tell them to love selflessly. Like a dog. Start with love… not biscuits."

"If you are lucky, the biscuits follow."

Conversations with my Dog

"Where are we today?"
"At a special place I've been wanting to show you."
"Then I'm glad we came. What are those sounds?"
"The deep, constant one you can hear is called 'the Sea' and the tinkly ones from high above our heads are little birds called skylarks."

"This place is full of magic!"
"How can you tell?"
"Because everything is sort of shimmering and trembling. Like it can't quite stay inside itself. The land, the sea and sky… it's hard to tell them apart here. It's like they are all one."
"Can you describe it in one word, Monty?"
"LIGHT!"

Conversations with my Dog

"This is a nice place to sit."
"Come on, Monty! I'm in a hurry!"
"Why?"
"Because we need to go!"
"Why do we?"

"Because we… Oh, hang on! You're right again. Maybe we should 'be here now'? I'm not really sure why we need to go. Not right now. So why are you sitting there on that wall?"
"It's nice. Come and try it?"

"OK, budge up. Hmm, so tell me, what are you doing up here?"
"I'm smelling for the stories of the land. The breeze is telling me what's going on. It helps to listen when you are on a journey."
"Right."

"Uh-huh. Down there in the lane, the breeze is kind of going over our heads, so all the stories are blowing by and getting lost. If I get up here I can read it. Don't you like to know what's going on?"
"Sure I do."
"Well, the smells on the breeze are kind of like the news humans listen to."

Conversations with my Dog

"Oh, wow!"

"What can you smell?"

"When I put my nose on the short grass I can smell the earth. It's warming up. I can smell different types of plants."

"What else?"

"The breeze is coming off the land, not the sea. That's quite unusual here. It smells of herbs. I can actually smell thyme!"

"Time? Even I can't smell that!"

"No… thyme."

"Oh never mind. Keep going!"

"How? I'm not a dog."

"Inhale more slowly. So that you aren't so much taking a deep breath as a slow breath. Take a breath at half the speed and this time let the air drift over the backs of your nostrils and ask what it is telling you. You might not have a dog's nose but you can still let the land tell you its stories. All you need is to take the thyme."

"You mean time."

"Whatever. Human words are so confusing. You're better off using your nose."

"I'm beginning to notice that! OK, I can smell flowers and streams, warm land and something that smells like rain but more stormy."

"Now you're getting it! How do you know the difference between the streams and the rain? They're both wet."

"I don't know. They're just different. The streams smell sort of colder and their scent is mixed up with the land. The rain is kind of on a different layer of smell, like melodies in a piece of music."

Conversations with my Dog

"You get it now?"

"Yes. I get it now. It's always worth taking the time to stop and breathe. To smell the air and notice what's around. We become more aware when we let the stories of the land tell us what's going on. If we are more aware, we make better journeys and it's easier to find our way home. Thanks Monty. Let's do this more."

"OK."

Conversations with my Dog

"So how can humans hear the stories of the land, Monty?"
"Breathe like a dog."
"Pardon?"
"Breathe slowly. Your nose is there to tell you things. That's why it's in front of you. To tell you where you are going. Stop and pay attention to the land and which way the breeze is blowing. If you ask, it will talk to you. Why don't all humans do that?"
"I think maybe they used to but they forgot."
"Oh. Well make sure you don't forget."
"OK."

"So do humans forget how to find their way home then?"
"Yes, a lot of times they do. They remember eventually, but often only they have made many, many journeys. They go the wrong way quite a lot."

"Sometimes they confuse each other too, by listening to other humans who haven't made enough journeys and are just as lost but pretending not to be."
"Maybe they should listen to a dog instead."
"I think so."

Conversations with my Dog

"Why do humans use so many words? Sometimes I can't hear the ones that matter, among all the extra ones."

"I've been wondering the same thing. I think because we have so many words we just get used to tossing them around like they don't matter."

"I don't have many words."

"That's OK. You communicate better without them."

Conversations with my Dog

"Does nothing ever worry you, Monty?"

"Sometimes, especially when things I don't know are bigger than me. But not for long when you're here. You make everything right. You are always bigger than the scary things and you know what to do."

"Thanks. There are some things I don't know if I can make right, Monty. Some things are bigger than me. Sometimes I'm scared, too."

"Well, maybe you just need to grow a bit more. I'm growing, so maybe you are too. Maybe we are growing together."

"Maybe you're right."

Conversations with my Dog

"You're far wiser than I am, Monty."
"What's 'wise'?"
"It's like knowing stuff in a really deep kind of way."
"You know lots! I don't even know what I know."
"Exactly!"

Conversations with my Dog

"Why are you tired?"

"Because we're still searching, Monty. Still hunting. We are still on this journey. It's turning into a much longer journey than I thought."

"That's OK. Some hunts are longer than others. Sometimes you don't always catch what you went looking for straight away. The pack has to hunt. It's life. Sometimes the pack has to get up and move, too. Sometimes it takes longer to find what they are looking for. Now and then they change their territory and make a new den somewhere else. It's just life."

"You're OK with that?"

"Sure. It's natural. I like exploring. It's how we learn. If we just stayed in the same place and did the same things we would never learn new games or better ways to find things we need. Being curious makes us more effective hunters."

"So we should have fun searching and see what we can learn?"

"That's right. We will find a good place to be. We will find a great new den."

"How do you know, Monty."

"I just do."

Conversations with my Dog

"So how do we find our new den, Monty? Where do you think it will be?"
"It's in the Infinite Tea! We just have to follow our noses."
"Great. Infinity is pretty large though, Monty. Could you narrow it down a bit? How do dogs find their way home? Or find a new home?"

"If I'm searching for something and I can't find it, it's because I either haven't looked well enough or maybe I'm looking in the wrong place.

"It's really important to not get distracted, too. If I search for your old sock, it's like it is calling to me, telling a story all about your toes, leather boots, muddy paths, sand and the soap you wash your feet with. If I'm following those and I suddenly think 'Rabbit!' then I might have fun chasing rabbit scent for a while but I won't find the sock I was looking for."

Conversations with my Dog

"So our new den is like an old sock?"
"Kind of. It will have a complex smell pattern, just like socks do."

"So the place that we are searching for is kind of making a picture of itself that I should be able to see in my mind?"
"Yes, just don't get distracted by rabbits!"
"OK, I'll try not to."

Conversations with my Dog

"Clear your mind, raise your nose to the air! Let it blow on the breeze to you, out of the Infinite Tea. What's out there? What do you smell? What pictures do you see?"

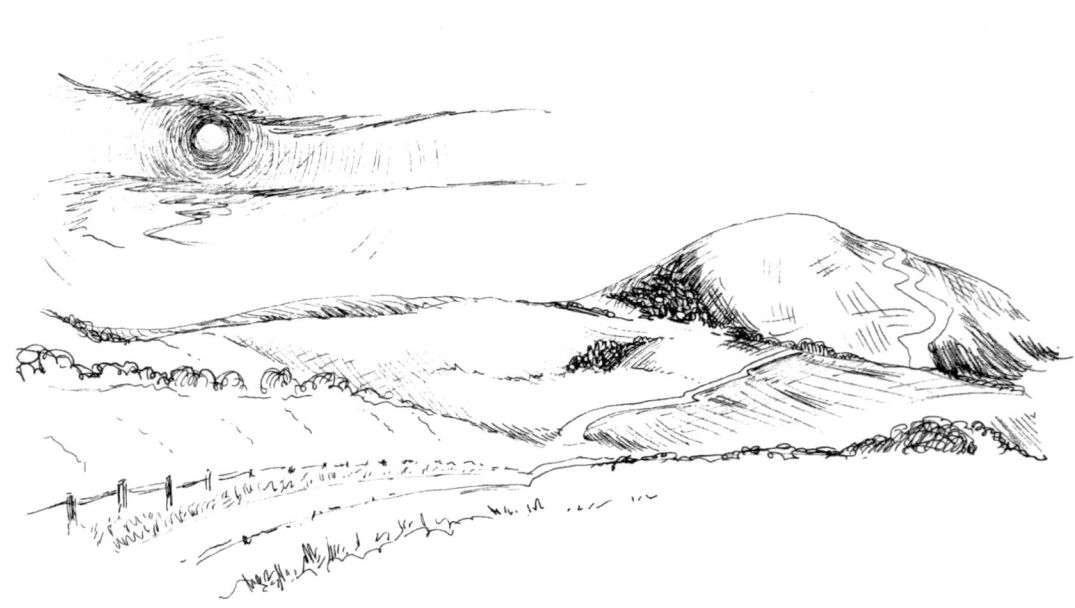

"Fresh air, water... short grass and high ground, the air is never still here... there are big birds high up circling on the wind... I can taste clean rain. We are near the sea. I can't see it but I know it's there somehow."

Conversations with my Dog

"Sometimes we discover the things we are looking for in places where we didn't expect to find them."

Conversations with my Dog

"Here's a place I think you'll like, Monty."
"It smells all wet… and kind of salty and strange. Whatever is it?"
"It's called a beach."
"It's AWESOME! It's so exciting!
"Do you like it?"
"WHEEEEEEE!!"

SPLOSH!

"What do you think?"
"WHEEEEEEEEEEEE!!!"

"This is SO MUCH FUUUUUUN!"

"I'm flyiiiing!"

"WHEEEEEE!"

Conversations with my Dog

"What would you do if you got lost, Monty?"

"How can I be lost? Lost to what? I'm in the Infinite Tea, so it has to know where I am because it's everywhere. I can lose something in it, or even lose my way, like going after a rabbit when I had started looking for a sock, but I can't be lost. You can't either."

"How about if I lost you?

"You'd find me and I'd find you! We'd 'be here, now' and then we'd meet up again. If we are Here and Now, aren't we together?"

"I see what you mean. But what about if we were travelling and we lost our way?"

"We would find a different way."

"Speaking of finding a new way, I've had an idea for somewhere new we could look for a den."

"Great! Is it near the sea? Does it have fresh, moving air, big birds and short grass?"

"I think so, yes."

"Let's go there now! Let's go and try it out."

Conversations with my Dog

"Why are you hesitating?"

"Because I don't know if it will work out for us in a new place, Monty."

"So why did you leave the old place?"

"Because it wasn't working out!"

"So you knew it was time to leave? You walked away from what didn't work?"

"Yes."

"Once we find a new place, will it be more like what you went looking for?"

"Yes."

"Then it will work out. Even if you took a chance. Sometimes the pack leader has to head for new places. Sometimes we have to cross a stream or go through woods to find a new den. We have to cross boundaries where we can't see the other side from where we are. If we just sat there looking at what was in the way, thinking about it, we would never find anywhere new. A lovely new den with lots of the most delicious biscuits could be just on the other side of a hill but if we never went forwards and just sat looking at the hill we wouldn't find it."

"So, sometimes we have to go through some woods or over a few hills to find what we are looking for?"

"Yup."

Conversations with my Dog

"Life doesn't sit still or go backwards. If we want to live, sometimes we have to move forwards. Even when we aren't sure of the way."

Conversations with my Dog

"Sometimes the reason things look different from how you expected they would is because of what you altered on the way.
The future changes for you every time you look at it down the path ahead and adjust course."

Conversations with my Dog

"I think sometimes we have more than one path running side by side, close to each other, because of things we started at one time or another and we are living on all of them for a while, where they meet up."

"Yup.…"

"Oh."

"Actually we always do. You just have developed the ability to see it."

"OH!"

"Sometimes those journey lines are stronger and the boundaries between them are thinner, so they are easier to sense, but they are always there; noticed or unnoticed. Most people are so preoccupied with being part of the pack they don't look up and ask which way the pack is running. You are a pack leader – so you have to be able to see the alternative paths."

"When did I become a pack leader?"

"When you said you would look after me and I said 'OK' and followed you."

Conversations with my Dog

"It seems like, sometimes, those lines get more entwined."
"I guess sometimes Time gets it's trouser legs tangled!"

Conversations with my Dog

"Sometimes people talk about being at a crossroads. But crossroads are easy. All you have to do is choose which way looks best. But being on multiple paths at the same time and knowing about it means that suddenly you know that it is you that creates the crossroads. That's a whole different ball game."

"Ooh! A ball game… now there's a good idea. Let's play?"

"Most times the pack doesn't recognise that there is a crossing point coming until they reach it. Finding the route there, like you are doing, is much more challenging."

"Like we are doing."

Conversations with my Dog

"Let's stop off here Monty. I've heard there is a nice place to look around and play".

"OK. Just getting out of the car… WOW! What's THIS?"

"This is a forest. A really big one!"

"Wow! Wow! There's so much of it. It's AMAZING! It looks like a great, green ocean over our heads. Does it go up to the sky?"

"Not quite, it's just very tall. It goes on for many miles."

"There must be everything in here. Maybe our den is in here!"

"I don't think so."

"Well let's look anyway. Let's explore. Let's go and have fun?"

"OK."

Conversations with my Dog

"This is a great place!"
"It is and it's much better because you are here with me."
"I'm sorry our den wasn't here."
"It's OK. We just came here to play."
"It's important to stop and play. It makes us better hunters. I like it here."
"If you could tell me in one word, what you like best about this place, Monty, what would it be?"
"MYSTERY!"

Conversations with my Dog

"When we find the den, then what will we do?"

"Oh my goodness! What a good question, Monty! What do you want to do?"

"Go on a new journey!"

"Really? Don't you want to stop travelling?"

"Nope."

"Why not?"

"Because you've taken me to places of mystery and light. When we travel we explore, learn and make new friends. I like doing all these things. Otherwise we would just stay the same, but we can't do that."

"Why not?"

"Because we are alive. Living things don't stay the same."

Conversations with my Dog

"We are companions on all our journeys. Not just one."

"So after we find a home, we have to keep finding new ways of exploring and learning?"

"Yes and making friends…

… Otherwise it won't be home. It will just be a place where we stopped growing."

Conversations with my Dog

"But our long journey will be over. Won't it? We will have found what we are looking for."

"I don't understand. This long journey is just a bit of searching and it will be over. But our Long Journey… well that goes on and on. Don't you know? I'm with you for all of it!"

"I thought journeys always had a beginning, a sort of long bit in the middle and then an end. You know, a time before the journey began and a time after it finished?"

"A time after our journey finishes? That doesn't make sense to me. There are many journeys within journeys."

"OK, fellow traveller, what will we search for next?"

"The way ahead…"

Conversations with my Dog

"You really are wiser than me! Is there always a way ahead?"

"Yes! All you have to do is look for it. Sometimes it's easy to find and other times it's hidden for a while but then you discover it. You just have to go a little further and it opens up."

"Like when we have to go to the right places on the edge of the cliffs to find the path to the sea?"

"Uh-huh. Sometimes there is a clear path and other times we have to run through tangly bits. You have to follow your nose!"

"And your heart… How do you know how to help me find the way Monty?"

"I can see the way ahead. It's much more than just what we see with our eyes."

"Dogs and humans have been travelling together for a long, long time."

"You're a great teacher, Monty…

… So, there are no real beginnings and endings. Right? We remember how to see the way ahead on the Big Journey when we stop going round in circles on the small ones?"

"Yes. Though it's often fun to do the small ones. Like hunting for a rabbit, a den or a sock. If that's what you need to do, then that's OK. Just be sure to remember which is which, so you don't get confused."

Conversations with my Dog

"We are here to travel together and learn from each other. Dogs have been guiding humans for a long time."

Conversations with my Dog

"You said you can see the way ahead. How do you do that?"
"I see with all my senses."
"Can I do it?"
"Of course! Why did you think you couldn't?"
"Dunno. I guess I was fitting in with the pack for too long."

"It happens. But you are Pack Leader now. You found us a new den too! It's time to follow your own lead and remember what you always knew."

Conversations with my Dog

"I'm happy to be sharing Home with you. Here in our new den! But you know what?"
"What?"

"I'm even more happy to have you to explore the Out There with!"

Conversations with my Dog

"I'm happy to be sharing our journey. Let's look forward to the way ahead and finding it together."

"The Out There is calling to us. Let's not keep it waiting!"

Conversations with my Dog

Conversations with my Dog